To Jonathan Bricklin, a bright light of his own kind

Special thanks to Dr. Betty Borowsky for her careful review of the text and illustrations in this book.

PHOTOGRAPHY CREDITS

Peter Arnold, Inc.: 10, Hans P. Fletschinger; 16, Manfred Kage; end-papers, Keith Kent; 18, Sea Studios, Inc.; cover, 24, 26, Norbert Wu.

Photo Researchers, Inc.: 5, 13, Bassot/Jacana; 21, Peter David; 9, W.K. Fletcher; 29, Peter Katsaros; 17, George Lower; 20, Tom McHugh; 22, Robert Noonan; 12, Steve Percival; 14, Dick Rowan; 28 (top), Kjell B. Sandved; 19, Stephen Spotte; 28 (bottom), Steinhart Aquarium/Tom McHugh; 7, 8, 11, 15, 23, 25, 27, Dr. Paul A. Zahl.

Concept and production by Brooke-House Publishing   Design by Diane Stevenson / SNAP · HAUS GRAPHICS
PUBLISHED BY DOUBLEDAY   a division of Bantam Doubleday Dell Publishing Group, Inc.   666 Fifth Avenue, New York, New York, 10103   DOUBLEDAY   and the portrayal of an anchor with a dolphin are trademarks of Doubleday,   a division of Bantam Doubleday Dell Publishing Group, Inc.   Library of Congress Cataloging-in-Publication Data: Barkan, Joanne.   Creatures that glow : a glow in the dark book / by Joanne Barkan.—1st ed.   p.   cm.   Summary: Introduces animals and plants that produce their own   light, from sea pens and fireflies to mushrooms. Includes   photographs that glow in the dark.   1. Bioluminescence—Juvenile literature.   2. Glow-in-the-dark   books—Specimens.   [1. Bioluminescence.   2. Glow-in-the-dark   books.   3. Toy   and   movable   books.]   I. Title.   QM641.B38 1991   574.19′125—dc20   91-7836
CIP   AC   ISBN 0-385-41978-3   ISBN 0-385-41979-1 (lib. bdg.)   R.L. 4.1   Text copyright © 1991 by Joanne Barkan
All Rights Reserved   Printed in the United States of America   October 1991   First Edition

CREATURES THAT GLOW

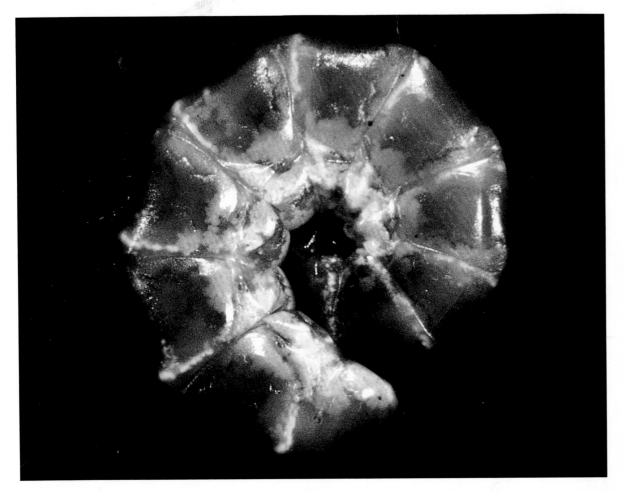

BY JOANNE BARKAN

DOUBLEDAY

NEW YORK • LONDON • TORONTO • SYDNEY • AUCKLAND

Contents

HOW AND WHY THEY GLOW

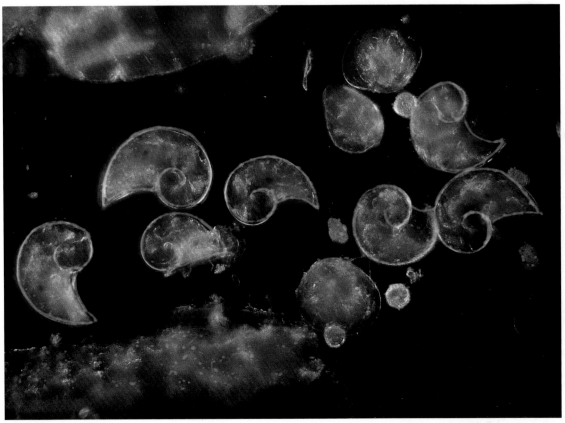

Marine organisms light up the waters near Puerto Rico.

THE glare of headlights on a deep-sea fish . . . the glow of a mushroom in the woods . . . the flashing beam of a firefly on a summer
night . . .

Where do these mysterious lights come from? You can flip a
switch, and—presto!—the electric light in your bedroom goes on. But
those fish, mushrooms, and fireflies aren't "plugged in." What makes
them light up?

It's bioluminescence (by-oh-loo-muh-NES-sense)—the production of light by living organisms.

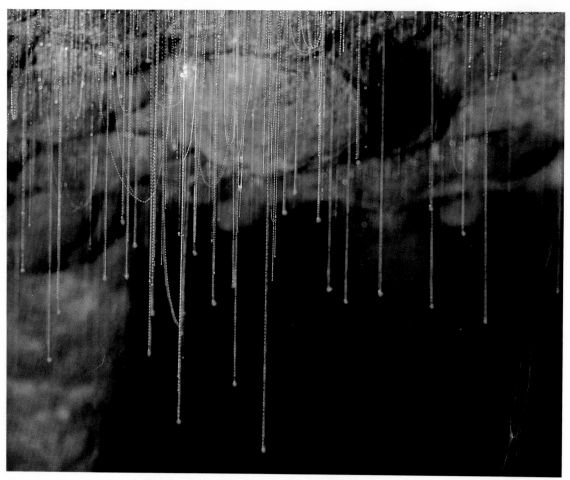

Glowworms dangle from filaments attached to the ceiling of a New Zealand cave.

You've probably seen fireflies blinking their lights in the grass. But you won't come across many other bioluminescent creatures on land. Aside from certain insects and funguses (a mushroom is a fungus), most kinds of glowing organisms live in the sea. In fact, thousands of them light up the inky darkness there.

No matter where they live, bioluminescent organisms glow because of a chemical process. Here's how it usually works: A substance called luciferin (loo-SIF-uh-run) reacts with oxygen in the presence of another substance, an enzyme called luciferase (loo-SIF-uh-raze). Chemical energy from the reaction is turned into light. Some organisms use different substances, but the process is always a chemical reaction that produces light.

These Malaysian fireflies gather in trees and blink on and off simultaneously.

If you lined up many different bioluminescent organisms, you'd see quite a rainbow of colors—blues, greens, yellows, reds. All of them, even the brilliant reds, are what scientists call "cold light." This means that if you held the glowing creatures in your hands, you would feel no heat. Unlike fire, which produces much heat and relatively little light, what the chemical reaction of bioluminescence produces is almost all light.

This glowing may be beautiful, but does it have a purpose? Actually, many bioluminescent organisms depend on their light to live. Some use it to see where they are going or to search for food. Some have elaborate glowing lures to draw in prey. For others, light is a fine defense—it can frighten away predators. Some fish confuse their enemies by zigzagging through the water and flashing their lights on and off. Just think how difficult it would be to catch that flitting light! Some creatures—fireflies are a good example—use light to attract a mate. But in many cases, scientists just don't know why an organism glows.

Bioluminescence usually isn't a steady light. Fireflies flash on and off. Some creatures glow only when stimulated—by a wave, by another creature, or perhaps by your foot. Some glow in the dark but fade in the light. Only funguses and microscopic bacteria glow all the time.

The fact that living things can generate light—no electrical wires or batteries needed—is an amazing phenomenon. Each bioluminescent organism has its own fascinating story. Let's explore some of them.

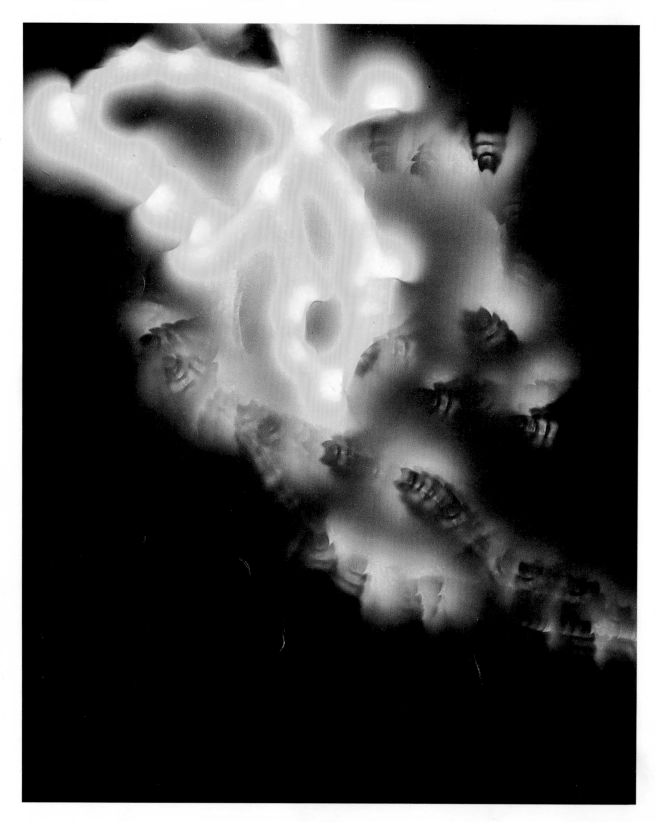

FIREFLIES

WHAT is the difference between a firefly and a lightning bug? There isn't any. The two names refer to the same insect. These creatures are actually soft-bodied beetles. At least 1,700 different species of fireflies live on earth. The one in the photograph on this page is a Jamaican firefly.

Males flash their lights as they fly. Females, who perch on or near the ground, flash back their own light signals. Males and females of the same species recognize each other by the number of flashes, the time between them, or the color of the light. They signal back and forth until a male joins a female.

There's only one firefly in the photograph on page 10. It was crawling on a sheet of film in a darkroom. As the insect moved about, its glow exposed the film—just the way you expose film to light when you press the shutter release of a camera. You could say that this firefly took a picture of itself with its own flash attachment!

GLOWWORMS

JUST as a firefly is not really a fly, a glowworm is not really a worm. The name "glowworm" is often used for the young of fireflies (larvae) and for the wingless females of some species of fireflies.

These two female glowworms are creeping across ice high in the mountains. We know that adult female glowworms attract mates with their light. But larvae don't need mates. No one really knows why those glowworms glow.

PHENGODES

HERE'S another group of soft-bodied beetles with a glittering display. Unlike their firefly and glowworm relatives, *Phengodes* don't limit their glow to the last segments of the abdomen. Instead, the wingless females and larvae flash a line of bright green lights along each side of their bodies. The beetle on this page is curled up in a circle.

So far we've looked at creatures that glow on land. Now let's explore the sea, home to most bioluminescent organisms.

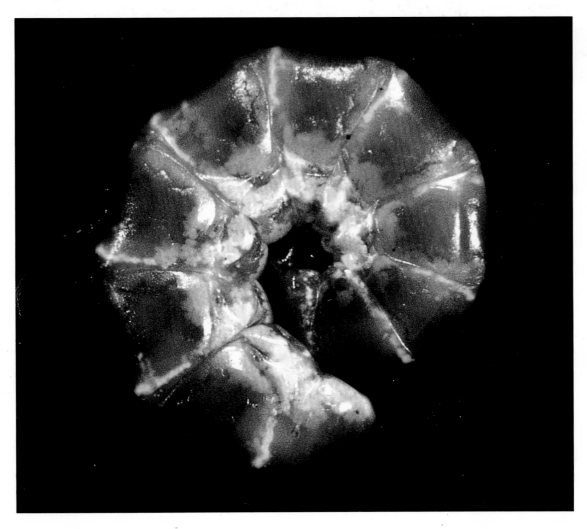

GLOWING SEAS

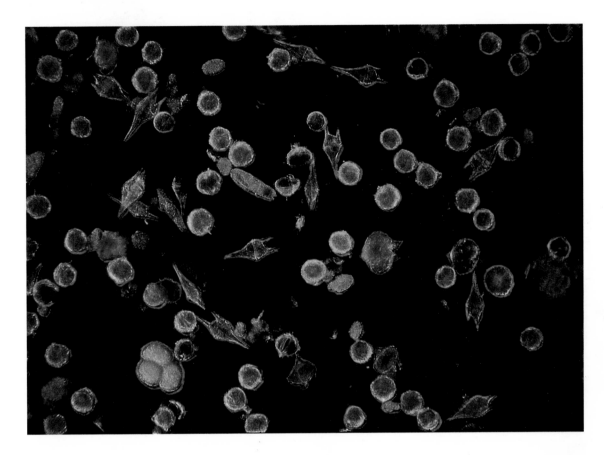

A BOAT glides through the sea, leaving behind a wake that gleams in the dark night. You run your hand through the water. It creates a trail of shimmering lights. Is it magic? To the naked eye, it's not clear what is causing the glow.

To solve the mystery, put a drop of the seawater under a microscope. There you'll see swarms of minute bioluminescent organisms. You're looking at tiny living lamps! Most are "turned on" by mechanical stimulation—the rocking of a boat, the thrust of a swimmer's hand, the motion of a fish, or even the sweep of a wave. Alone, each organism gives off a weak glow. But when millions swim together, they can make the oceans glitter with magical light.

NOCTILUCA

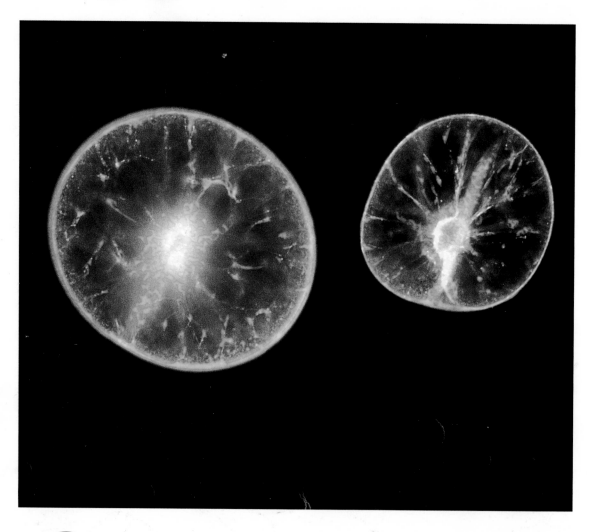

ONE group of tiny lamps is called *Noctiluca* (NAHK-tuh-LOO-kuh). *Noctiluca* are protozoa, a form of life made up of a single cell. Mechanical stimulation lights up these organisms, but only at night. They seem to have an invisible clock—an internal biological clock—that tells them when to glow.

Some scientists think protozoa use their light to confuse predators. Other scientists aren't sure why the little lamps glow. For these organisms and many others as well, light might be a beautiful but purely accidental product of another chemical reaction.

SEA WALNUTS

I F you explore the ocean at night, you might see broad patches of light that seem to be created by transparent blobs of jelly. These are sea walnuts, creatures that belong to a larger group of animals called comb jellies. Some sea walnuts grow to be four inches long.

Look at the radiating lines of light along a sea walnut's body. Each line is covered with many tiny hairlike strands called cilia (SIL-ee-uh). Touch the cilia, and structures underneath them will immediately produce light. The cilia will seem to glow.

BEROE'S COMB JELLY

THIS reddish comb jelly is less transparent than a sea walnut, and its shape is more oval. But like a sea walnut, its body is divided by loops of glowing cilia.

All comb jellies have gaping mouths at one end of their bodies. As they swim along, they swallow up food. What they're eating is plankton—masses of microscopic organisms that live near the water's surface. A glowing comb jelly's food might include some glowing *Noctiluca*.

SEA PEN

FAR below the water's surface, in the mud or sand on the ocean floor, that's where you'll usually find sea pens. They look like swollen feathers or puffy plants, but don't be fooled. Each sea pen is really a large colony of fleshy, simple animals called polyps (PAHL-ips). (Corals and sea anemones, too, are polyps.) A sea pen feeds on bits of food carried in the currents of water.

Some sea pens are just one inch high; others grow to be three feet tall. Like the one on this page, most of them glow in the dark. If anything touches a sea pen, light will pass over the creature from one polyp to the next, like a wave.

PARCHMENT TUBE WORM

THIS marine worm lives like a hermit. It hides away in a tube made of a parchment-like membrane and buries itself in the sand. Despite these precautions, the worm is sometimes disturbed. When that happens, many gland cells on its body secrete a glowing slime.

Some scientists doubt that the bioluminescence serves a specific purpose for the parchment tube worm. But others speculate that the light might ward off enemies like the eel.

DEEP-SEA SQUID

YOU'LL probably recognize this scene: A threatened squid ejects a cloud of black ink and then jets away from its confused enemy. Now imagine a cloud of glowing slime instead of black ink. Some squids have light organs that produce a luminous secretion. They eject this in order to make an escape.

Many deep-sea squids are bioluminescent. Some have light organs on the ends of their tentacles; some have them on their eyes. The three-inch-long squid on this page has small light organs all over its body.

FRESHWATER LIMPET

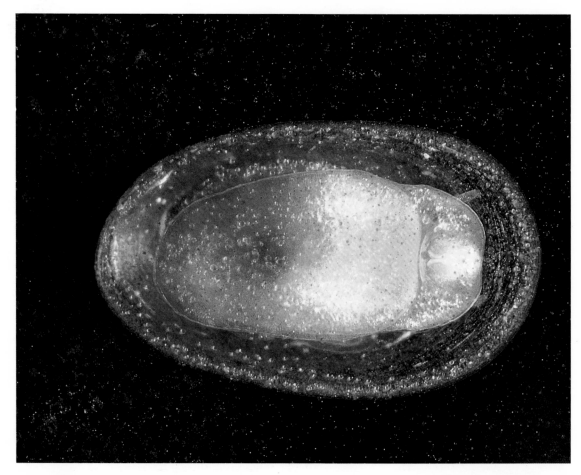

ALL the aquatic creatures we've looked at so far make their homes in the saltwater oceans. This limpet, however, lives in fresh water. In fact, it's one of just two freshwater bioluminescent animals known to exist on earth. (The other is the larva of a particular firefly.) The glowing freshwater limpet is found in New Zealand.

Limpets have conical shells to protect their soft bodies. The one on this page has been photographed from underneath while feeding on algae. You can see its luminescence and the broad, muscular "foot" that allows it to cling to rocks when it's not feeding.

LANTERN FISH

EVERY evening, schools of tens of thousands of lantern fish rise from the ocean depths to shallower waters. Pearly light organs glow on snouts, near eyes, and on the sides and lower parts of their small bodies. (Most lantern fish are three to six inches long.) Each species—and there are more than 220 of them—has its own arrangement of light organs. Lantern fish probably use these brilliant patterns to recognize their own species.

The "lanterns" also serve to attract prey, and as camouflage. When an enemy swims below a lantern fish, it sees dappled light above that matches the sunlight or moonlight filtering through the water.

ANGLER FISH

THIS deep-sea creature fishes for food. Its flexible rod (actually a modified fin ray) ends in a light organ. When trying to catch some dinner, the angler dangles the glowing bait right in front of its mouth. An unsuspecting fish swims up for a closer look and—*snap!*—the angler's huge jaws snatch up the prey.

Angler fish are small, but they can be big eaters. A three-and-a-half-inch angler was found with a lantern fish almost twice that size inside its stretchable stomach!

HATCHET FISH

THIS strange image is the underside of a hatchet fish. The wider end is its head; in the center, you can see two fins; then its body tapers down toward the tail. As you look through the translucent body, notice the parallel rows of light organs with their pink pigment.

There are two types of light organs in fish. Some fish have "true" light organs (or photophores) that produce light by means of a chemical reaction. The light organs of other fish are really structures filled with bioluminescent bacteria.

The hatchet fish has true photophores. They contain photogenic (light-producing) tissue, pigment, color filters, lenses, and reflectors. They function like theater spotlights on a very miniature scale.

FLASHLIGHT FISH

MILLIONS of bacteria fill the light organ under each eye of the flashlight fish. The bacteria glow all the time, but the fish can blink its beams on and off. How is that possible? The light organs are hinged. They roll back into a groove—and then out goes the light.

A flashlight fish and its bacteria have a symbiotic relationship. This means they both benefit from it. The bacteria receive nutrients and oxygen from the fish's blood. In return, the fish gets a light organ. Scientists think the light attracts both prey and mates. And when an enemy appears, the flashlight fish escapes by zigzagging through the water, blinking its light.

BACTERIA

HERE'S a closer look at light-generating bacteria. In fact, you're seeing *billions* of them glowing in one small dish. Of all the tiny living lamps in the world, bioluminescent bacteria are the tiniest. They give off a steady bluish light of the same intensity, day and night. Scientists have found that bacteria like these, grown in a laboratory, make good material for studying bioluminescence. But in spite of all they've discovered, scientists still don't know why these bacteria glow.

FLUORESCENCE
(NOT BIOLUMINESCENCE)

THESE corals glow in the dark with jewel-like colors. Another spectacular example of bioluminescence? No, the corals are fluorescing (floor-ES-ing).

Many corals glow when exposed to ultraviolet light—a short-wave light that humans can't see. (Bioluminescent organisms don't need light to glow.)

Suppose you went scuba diving in the ocean at the depth where the water blocks out all visible light, and only ultraviolet rays can penetrate. You would see corals fluorescing brilliantly. If you brought those corals into the daylight, they would immediately turn drab shades of brown. Shine an artificial ultraviolet light on them, and they would blaze again with rich color.

ORANGE MILKCAP MUSHROOM

LEAVING the ocean, we find a final example of bioluminescence close to home: the mushroom. This particular species—the orange milkcap—grows in the hardwood forests of the eastern half of the United States.

Scientists have found no true plants that produce light. But some species of funguses are bioluminescent. Some funguses are tiny—for example, yeast and mold. When a fungus has a stalk and a cap, it's called a mushroom.

Not all mushrooms glow. The sliced ones on top of your pizza don't. But when a mushroom does generate light, it gives off a steady glow all the time. No one knows the purpose of a mushroom's light. For now, it too remains one of the mysteries of bioluminescence.